DEDICATION

I dedicate this to all those that left the many scars on my mind, heart and soul.

Without you, I wouldn't have realised my strength and without you I wouldn't be writing this for all my fellow damaged souls out there. XOX

GABRIELLA LEONARDI

. . . .

The Art of a Damaged Soul

AUSTIN MACAULEY PUBLISHERS™

LONDON • CAMBRIDGE • NEW YORK • SHARJAH

A CIP catalogue record for this title is available from the British Library.

ISBN 9781398440982 (Paperback)
ISBN 9781398440999 (ePub e-book)

www.austinmacauley.com

First Published (2021)
Austin Macauley Publishers Ltd
25 Canada Square
Canary Wharf
London
E14 5LQ

FOREWORD

by Gabriella Leonardi

The Art of a Damaged Soul is aimed as a therapeutic poetry book for those that often feel alone, lost, heartbroken and down. This is written for anyone to look at when their heart may be hurting, their mind may be dark or their soul feels empty. The contents of this book range from poems to quotes to essentially anything inspired by feelings. I would argue that included is everything a 'damaged soul' would feel. Everyone uses different forms of art to express their feelings and who they are; therefore, each and every soul would seek comfort in this book. We all have our own traumas and experiences that others don't understand. Art is an incredible form of expression as it allows us all to relate to one another; to understand our own trauma, heartbreak, sadness and loneliness. Even though our own experience is unique, finding something that understands even a fraction of that, makes you feel unified, not alone and as if someone, somewhere understands. I believe *The Art of a Damaged Soul* does just that.

When I had the idea to write this, I was curled up in a ball on my bed, hadn't left my room for two days and had only eaten two bowls of Coco Pops with almond milk in that time. For two straight days I cried so hard. You know the cry when it is full of so much hurt, you feel your heart shattering and you are crying with so much force yet no sound comes out, just an occasional whimper. I thought to myself in that moment, *I have no fucking idea what I am doing, who I am, where I belong or what my purpose in life is.* I felt like I had no purpose and just wanted to walk to the cliff ten minutes from my house and just jump; at least then I'd feel like I was flying, just for a second. I have felt like this so many times and just ended up sitting on the cliff for hours watching the waves, but I knew this time was different and I might not have been strong enough to just sit there that time. I wondered if anyone else was feeling this way, so broken and hurt with no hope for the future. So, instead, I started to write and add to it for an entire week. A week where I didn't leave my room, not even to be outside with nature, something I love so deeply... and that is this book, everything I wrote in that week that then led onto a year's worth of editing and writing.

I know even when you are reading this, if this ever gets published and I am able to share this with all the other souls out there, whether it be six months, a year, five or ten years, I will still be hurting and I won't be magically cured. Life doesn't work that way, you don't just write it down and everything will be fixed; but I will be **alive.** I will be surviving this mad world and fighting the demons inside my mind, constantly searching for the stars to break the darkness away. I will be hoping to hear your thoughts, your stories, your trauma and pain which I think is your **ART.** It is **The Art of a Damaged Soul.** *Your* damaged soul. It is beautiful, it is raw. It is what makes you who you are and you should never have to feel ashamed of your scars. I genuinely believe the most beautiful and brightest of souls are the ones with the most scars. The ones that are the most damaged. I guess I hope this book not only allows you to find hope and peace within yourself but also to inspire you to keep going, to keep surviving and fighting every day to survive.

I started this book the first week of June 2020, when we were living through a global pandemic and a historical revolution. Although it was such a dark time, it wasn't those two things that caused my trauma and scars; it just made me be alone with a lot of time on my hands to realise the hurt and pain I had been carrying over the years when I was trying all this time to block it out. At this time I had been in lockdown for fourteen weeks, desperately trying to stay productive and fighting the darkness that was filling my mind, heart and soul.

I hope that this book allows you to have the courage to be open about who you are and your story. I hope it resonates with you and allows you to manifest all your biggest dreams and desires. I really hope it helps you get up and live a life you want to live and to continue to Be Brave, Be Bold and Be Beautiful in your own unique way, not in a way society makes us believe we have to be. I am not a 'writer' as such; I always got bad grades in English for my punctuation and grammar but everything you are about to read is real. It is raw. I decided to submit it to be published in the hope to make a difference to at least just one person's life. To remind someone that you are worthy and it is OK to be whoever you want to be.

So this is for all the damaged souls out there, wherever in the world you may be.

I hope you enjoy this book and I'd love to hear your thoughts.

This is The Art of a Damaged Soul.

Never-ending love and bravery,

Gabriella Leonardi x

ACKNOWLEDGEMENTS

Thank you to all those that have been there for me through my darkest moments, you know who you are. I want to especially thank Lucy for getting me through drama school and the darkest period of my life to date. We don't talk much anymore but you showed me I had more fight left in me to make it through and that I will find my happiness no matter what life throws at me or how dark life gets. I hope you find your happiness too, Lucy, as without you, I wouldn't have been here to write this book.

CONTENTS

The World

The Heart

The Mind

The Soul

In no particular order, just all jumbled up like the thoughts inside our mind, the feelings inside our heart and the sensations in our soul.

A Tale of a Damaged Soul

. . . .

I think there comes a point, for even the strongest of souls, where they can no longer fight the never-ending battle for happiness.

For this damaged soul realised there were far too many scars for her to continue on. For her insecurities and fear would absorb her and they would form a monster.

That monster would eventually consume her and lead her to the path everyone knew would eventually come. For then, she would finally be at peace and free of that monster as the monster cannot travel beyond the living.

Of course, her memory on earth would live on in others' minds as they eventually get back to their normal lives. They will always wonder if things would have been different if they tried a little harder, but deep down they knew her fate was sealed.

I'm sure you're used to fairytales and stories filled with happily-ever-afters. Perhaps you're used to the movies where the victim fights and fights without giving up and wins at the end.

This isn't a fairytale or an inspiring movie. This is a dark painful tale about a damaged soul who was far too sensitive. She was a beautiful, fragile, timid being who couldn't fight off the darkness that consumed her in this cruel unjust world. She was misunderstood and no one had the patience to help her heal. We are all too focused on ourselves, as that is what it takes to survive in such a dangerous, dark world.

You will agree, I'm sure. Why else would you have continued to read such a dark and twisted tale, knowing it was a true story? We love the darkness... we are slaves to it. That is why after this you will scroll through Netflix and watch a documentary or series about a serial killer or robotically scroll through your social media feed and make yourself question your worth. All I will say is try and be the damaged soul that survives... no matter how sensitive and fragile you are.

Damaged

. . . .

Why do we look at this word and think it is such an awful thing?

My love, we are all so damaged, that is what makes us human.

Damaged, is what makes us beautiful, raw and real.

So here is to the art of being.

The Art Of Being A Damaged Soul.

Untitled

. . . .

I guess I realised I was different when I saw everyone having fun and instead of smiling and laughing with them I was holding back my tears.

I knew that with my past, combined with my present worries and insecurities, it would always be difficult to enjoy my future years.

I have come to realise that pain makes you quiet and it is in the silence one realises one's deepest darkest fears.

One day, maybe I too, will be able to feel real happiness?

The Little Things

. . . .

I realised love is not what the movies teach us. The chocolates, the flowers, the candlelit gourmet meals and the expensive clothes. I realised, when I met him, these things are momentary. The food will be devoured, the flowers die and the clothes will be phased out with the change of fashion or the change of our bodies.

I realised when I met him, that love is what some may call 'the little things'. The cuddles at night and the way he wraps his arm around you first thing when you both wake up. The kisses and the reassuring glances. The massages when you're hurting after a long work day or the way he kisses your spots and bumps. The constant checking up on you. "Are you OK? How are you feeling? Do you need anything?"

Do you need anything? Not do you need overly priced chocolates, fancy gourmet candlelit meals or designer items. No. It's *Do you need a coffee, a glass of water, a cuddle, support and advice? Do you need reassurance or for me to remind you you're beautiful and that I love you?*

Yes, treats here and there are beautiful. When you come home from a long, awful day and there's your favourite vegan chocolate waiting on the bed with your favourite coffee or the coconut water that you love so much. When you come home and he is cooking dinner for you because he cares and he knows you've had a bad day.

I realised when I met you, my love, that love is all about the little things. Life filled with many little beautiful gestures, looks, cuddles and kisses. You made me feel unconditional love and for that I'm eternally grateful. So when your day is hard after building an empire filled with your hopes and dreams, I will be there too, waiting for you, with the little things that make you feel loved.

A Combination of the Sun and the Moon

. . . .

You are my sunshine, for you light up the dark cloud that has surrounded me for so long. Your light represents hope, safety, comfort and love. I hope I can be your moonlight that brings out the truth inside your soul. I hope, just like the mystery that lies amongst the moon, I can show you it is OK to feel. I hope we feel together and balance each other out. You can light my path with your sunlight and I'll light your path with the moonlight and eventually our two paths shall meet and become one, and as one they shall stay. Then, together as one, we can build our world and follow the single path to our home.

Guard

· ·

She had her guard up to protect her heart, mind and
soul. Little did she know her guard would then, over
time, form the darkest hole. It would be buried deep
inside her skin and if she didn't let her guard down the
darkness would soon win.

Said the Miner

. . . .

The miner said, "Just love me baby, stop fighting this," as I listened whilst realising the miner's love is poison and it has been consuming my soul.

"You're damaged, baby, stop ruining your future with your past," said the miner whose heart was in fact darker than the dirtiest piece of coal.

"There's no one else, baby, it's in your head. Stop being crazy, baby," said the miner whose lies were digging the biggest hole.

Yet still I want to be blinded by love and not accept the truth as I stand in the rain and watch him through the window with her, the girl whose name I still do not know.

Said the Gold

. . . .

The gold said, "Please. I can't breathe, eat, drink or sleep without knowing the truth," as he listened and started to spin his web of lies.

"I don't know what I did wrong for you to cheat, lie and treat me this way," said the gold as she was on her knees begging, her words muffled from the heartbroken cries.

"Just tell me how to improve, what to change about myself and I'll be better," said the gold whilst he was secretly in between another girl's thighs.

She had no idea that she didn't need to change, for she was the most precious bit of gold, and that she must walk away from the miner before her golden soul dies.

Blindfold

. . . .

He wore his lies so well. So well, that even once she knew the truth, she trained her mind to forget it. For hope was a dangerous thing and he trained her to wear her blindfold, so very well.

Eventually

. . . .

Walking away from you will be the hardest thing I will
ever do.

North Laines

. . . .

I'm sat here in a pub in the North Laines watching the Brightonions pass by and I can't help but hold my tears in for there are so many reasons to cry.

I know I should be grateful I'm alive and I am here walking on this Earth, but I can't help but think perhaps I've been depressed since birth.

I know this can't be so for this is not possible but I fear the depression growing in my mind is unstoppable.

So as I sit at my table with my vegan burger and my notebook, I begin an attempt to share my story hoping to give readers a better outlook.

So here's to a better outlook on our life no matter how dark the past has been, perhaps we should start by casting our eyes up from our phone screen.

I'm sat here in a pub in the North Laines watching the Brightonions pass by, and through my tears I hope I can write a book to remind others that it's not their time to die.

To My Narcissistic Ex

. . . .

To think for seven months I was just a puppet on a string, yet all I wanted from you the entire time was the simplest thing.

I wanted your time, loyalty, safety and love, yet I didn't get any of the four listed above.

You told me you were working so hard all the time, and you wanted me to stay home cook/clean and I said, "Fine."

After all you told me it was for a home that together we shall build, little did I know to protect myself from you I'd need a fucking strong shield.

You told others I was your colleague and we weren't together, whilst I lay in our bed and you tell me I'm your forever.

How could you lie so easily and look me in the eye, how does my heart cope knowing the past seven months was just a big lie?

I never asked for much, I just wanted to be in your arms; you told me you'd always protect me from harm.

I didn't realise the whole time you would be the one to destroy me, but your lies cast like a blindfold not allowing me to see.

You made me isolate myself from everyone around, and so through the abuse not once did I make a sound.

I find out you cheated, not just once but 18 times, and the only way I can express this is through these words and these rhymes.

You made everyone believe you were this handsome Prince Charming, and no one could see the girl in your bed you were harming.

I moved my whole life for you and now I'm in this city sat alone, and I'm comparing myself to the other girls I now search on my phone.

What did I do to you to make you gaslight me and harm me this way? I always tried to leave you but every time you begged me to stay.

So through my poetry I wanna scream why didn't you just let me go?! Instead of knowing you were making me feel the lowest of low.

Does destroying a girl make you feel better inside? Well, when people see the real you, you better hide.

You may have got away with it now but you won't for long, because the abuse you have committed is so fucking wrong.

I won't tarnish your name like you did with mine, nor shall I wear a mask like you are and pretend I'm fine.

I'm not ashamed to show the hurt and pain that I feel,
but you should be scared for when I finally heal.

Because when I do you will watch me when I'm back on a
high, and envy how strong I am and how tall I shall rise.

Abusers like you never truly win, and one day you will
pay for your sick dirty sin.

So for all those who are listening to this, a word to
the wise: follow your gut when you think your man's
between another girl's thighs.

He may say you're crazy, delusional and mad, but it's
just a method to keep you sad.

For when you are sad you're more likely to stay through the abuse, but my advice to you is cut your abuser loose.

So for all those that are listening, this is another word to the wise, you are beautiful and the strength you have found through your abuse is a fucking incredible prize.

& rise you will.

Toast to Death

· ·

Tonight we toast to death, for without the certainty of death we will never truly appreciate the value of life. We will just survive rather than truly live.

Silence

I now understand, after feeling so much pain, why the silence is so piercing. It is louder than the hustle and bustle in the cities, the sirens of all emergency vehicles and ten thousand people talking so loud without listening to others.

It is in the silence, we realise our darkest thoughts, worries and concerns.

The Mind

· ·

A hurricane of emotions.

A cloud of confusion.

A tornado of worry and frustration.

A cobbled path of memories.

A long shelf of jars filled with dreams.

A padlocked box of love and heartbreak.

A photo frame of hope.

A once clean but now extremely dirty bath of trauma.

A house filled with arguments.

A bed full of passion.

A closet of labels and identities.

A snow globe of endless adventures and travels.

A time bomb filled with anger.

A soundtrack of voices, feelings, thoughts.

A movie of life choices.

A social media platform filled with both new and lost connections.

A notebook of mistakes.

A photo album of insecurities.

A mind filled with all of the above.

The mind.

The Heart

. . . .

It can never be truly explained, nor truly and entirely
understood.
That is what makes it such a beautiful organ.

It is the size of your fist but it can hold a never-ending
amount of feelings and emotions.
It's many layers of tissue, acting as thick walls and
barriers, desperately trying to protect itself.

The heart, a magnificent creation.

Less

I was your moon; she then became your moon too, that shone a little brighter and so you chose her.

Perhaps it was because she was less damaged?

In Another Life?

. . . .

I'm holding hands with your heart,
knowing that our love will forever stay.

Your eyes see through my soul,
making me want to live another day.

Deep down I knew something was wrong but
Little did I know, that this was just pretend

Your heart belonged to someone else
And I was only ever worthy of being your friend.

I'm holding hands with your heart,
Wishing our love was strong enough for you to stay.

Your eyes pierce through my soul,
As you watch me walk away.

Goodbye; Maybe in another life?

Beautiful

· ·

What does it mean to be beautiful, my little sister asked
me one day,
I didn't know how to answer, at first I didn't know what
to say.
I think it means to be kind, be gentle and sweet,
And respect everyone in your life, that you'll eventually
come to meet.

It doesn't mean how you look, the shape of your body or
features on your face,
To be beautiful is to have a kind soul and learn how to
deal with your mistakes.
Of course some people in this world will be unkind and
cruel,
And you will of course encounter much of this at school.

So to be beautiful is to deal with the trauma and pain
that will come your way,
And channel your feelings, thoughts and emotions
without turning your soul grey.

To me, beauty should be found deep in your soul,
And that, my dear sister, should be the ultimate goal.

You are beautiful and oh so pretty, you are so gorgeous,
so kind,
And many will see your looks, but not many will
understand your mind.
So if you aim to be beautiful, make sure you are content
with yourself,
And never ever compare or wish to be someone else.

When you grow up people will tease you, bully you and
be mean,
And my advice to you is don't spend so much time
behind your phone screen.
Social media exists and it can make you have high
expectations,
And make your mind, heart and soul feel many
sensations.

The important thing in life is to have genuine human connections,
In a world where everyone is so obsessed with their reflections.
So my beautiful sister, live life to the full and be brave,
Do what you want and be who you want, never be society's slave.

What does it mean to be beautiful, my little sister asked me one day,
At first I didn't know how to answer but now I know what to say.
My sister, in this cruel world people will tell you how you should be,
But to be beautiful is to be unique, strong, brave, kind and free.

Soul and Skin

· ·

Take care of your soul, darling, it's more sensitive than your skin.
Yet we focus more on what can be seen rather than what lies within.

Only I

Only I would find the monsters hidden amongst the constellations of beautiful stars.

Oceans

· ·

I am someone with an ocean of dreams building inside
me. The waves and storms build up inside my soul. One
day you will witness the waves crash upon the shore and
make its mark for all to see.

He

. . . .

He says a world without crazy isn't a world for him. Well
for that I am glad because my mind is beyond crazy.

Naive

. . . .

She was naive. She didn't want to believe that yet another person would be capable of being so cruel?

She was naive. She didn't think she'd ever be a victim of the dark abuse cases she once got taught about in school.

The Blackboard was Handed the Chalk

We live in a world where it is so easy to stalk,
even a phone can track where one may walk.

We live in a world where it is so easy to stalk,
We don't know who is listening, as we talk.

He belonged in a world where it is easy to stalk,
His eyes beady, claws sharp, just like a hawk.

To explain this dark tale and tell you in short
This is what the police wrote in their report.

They named him the blackboard
and her social media was the white chalk.

Hextalls Lane

· ·

There was a place we drove past that went by the name of Hextalls Lane, and since that day things have never been the same.

I knew from the start that to love is to accept what we create could be lost, but I didn't believe our dreams would come at such a cost.

I hope we both find the right paths that we seek, and one day in the future we will again meet...

We will realise we are a beautiful storm and our love is as pure as the rain, and together we will drive down the cute place that went by the name of Hextalls Lane.

ECG

. . . .

I had an ECG: they checked how I breathe and said
I should find more reasons to survive.

Little did they know my mind is much more damaged
than my heart.

Temporary

· ·

Just like my spots are to my skin, I am the same to you...

temporary.

Hide

· ·

Some days I want to hide myself away from the world.
I don't want to infect the world with my darkness.

Was It?

....

I am not where you left me but don't come back when
you finally see.

After all, love is blind but was it even love?

Sugar

. . . .

I remember. I remember how many sugars you used to put in your coffee or how you'd tip the sugar bag into your bowl of porridge because the thought of sweet things touching your ever-so-bitter soul was nice for you. The sugar worked as a mask, a mask you wore so well.

Salt

· ·

The salt from your tears are in fact crystals which are being released to begin your journey of healing. So cry. Cry as much as your body allows.

Hi Reader,

This is a reminder that you are beautiful.

This is a reminder that you are brave.

If I Was to Have a Child

· ·

Maybe if I was to have a child and it was a little girl,
I would call her journey and show her to the world.

Her name would be a symbol for all she will achieve,
if she sets her mind to it and she will always continue to
believe.

That her entire life will be a journey full of all things bad
and good,
even though often in her life she will be misunderstood.

One day I will tell her, just like her father always told me, life is a beautiful journey and you deserve to be wild, young, loved and free.

Sleepville

Sleep well in sleepville.

You will find me there waiting for you, next to all your hopes and dreams and I'll be there with a coffee for us both, standing underneath the rain cloud so we can dance and kiss in the rain and feel not only the rain but each other's hands on our skin once again and we will stay there forever, happy and free.

The Mystery of Pain

. . . .

The mystery of pain. If you think about it too much it drives you insane, right?

Ray of Light

· ·

I'm supposed to be your ray of light but I can't help but feel I am no longer the moon that lights up the sky of your mind, or perhaps I never really was?

I'm supposed to be your ray of light but the truth is that's not me, it's as if I'm falling asleep at the wheel of the car and I am about to tumble off the road and end our journey.

I'm supposed to be your ray of light and if you believe I am, then my love I ask you to wake me up before I end all I've ever wanted because of the fear you'll end it first.

You're the only thing I'm sure of, so come closer, unravel me and let my damaged mind love you like I do because I love you more than anything in this world. It's the one thing I'm sure of and in you I have finally found my home.

The Vulnerable

....

"Love me."

– She begged.

The Hunter

. . . .

" I do, baby."

– He lied.

Ugly

. . . .

It is 2020 and there is so much ugly in the world, so be the change.

I am serious...

Enough of all this U G L Y.

When You Can Live in a World...

· ·

When you can live in a world with no danger,
and you can walk the streets alone.
When you can trust a random stranger,
Without trying to hide your phone.

When you can live in a world with no danger,
And you leave others alone.
When you can trust a random stranger,
Without fearing you may not see your young fully grown.

When you can live in a world with no hunger,
Yet our animals can still run free.
If we had known this when we were younger,
We could have protected our sea.

When you can live in a world with no hunger
and both animal and human can live free.
If we had known this when we were younger,
Oh how much happier we would be.

Baby

. . . .

If someone took your baby,
yet you looked after it so well,
You'd go absolutely crazy,
You'd feel as though you were in hell.

Yet you take that animal's baby,
and feed it to your child.
And some will call me crazy,
but that baby belongs in the wild.

Here's a lesson to teach your baby,
Animal or human – kidnap is wrong.
So perhaps that means that, maybe,
All babies deserve the chance to grow up strong.

So stop the slaughter and the stealing,

and let's all live together as one.

And let the earth start its healing,

Or one will turn to none.

If the World Is Round

. . . .

If the world is round, how on earth can I get off when I want to?

If the world is round, how do you expect me to escape without passing the pain to others?

If the world is round, why have they not invented a way to escape and get off for just a second?

If the world is round, how on earth can I leave… but be able to come back if I change my mind?

I'm not an astronaut.

Silent Scream

You're at the table,
Shivering in the house with no heating.
You feel like your throat is being scratched apart;
not sure whether it's the allergy to your mother's cats
or the dark monster inside of you scratching away and
he's made his way to your throat.

You scream a silent scream that fills the silent air,
with nothing but sadness and fear.
You scream so loud inside,
Yet no one can hear.
You scream a silent scream,
Hoping the one you need is near.

Yet I remain strong and hope for a better tomorrow.

One of Those Days

It was just one of those days,
Where I wake up and my heart is empty.
I try to think of different ways,
to fill it up again and feel whole.

It's just one of those days,
Where I miss you so deeply.
I try to find my way out of the maze,
And find my way back to you.

It's just one of those days,
Where I wish I could turn back time.
Perhaps I could then find different ways,
To make my life work with you.

It's just one of those days,
Where I want to hold you close.
I try to convince myself it's just a phase,
And that it will go away.

It's just one of those days,
Where I try to hold back the tears,
I try to find my way out of the haze,
Whilst praying we will be OK.

But it was just one of those days,
When I couldn't find the words to say.
So I let you slip away,
And my world turned the deepest shade of grey.

Praying

. . . .

I find myself praying to a god I don't believe in, praying
he can be my eyes and prove to me I am not crazy and
paranoid like you say.

Healing

. . . .

The more tiring part of being a damaged soul, is how
hard it is to start the process of healing. Yet once
we finally realise we are worthy to heal, we will be
unstoppable.

Almond Milk

. . . .

The darkness greets me with my morning coffee and cereal.

I stare at my bowl. The Coco Pops just as dark as the monster that slowly consumes my soul.

I watch as the chocolatey darkness creeps out and infects my almond milk.

Frozen

It's always the worst in the morning when you realise it's not a nightmare and you feel paralysed in your bed and can do nothing but blankly stare.

Shadows

. . . .

Your touch left scars on my soul and the traces of you
follow me like my shadow.
I did not consent.

Cologne

· ·

Perhaps you know the scars have truly consumed you when you're in a room full of people and have never felt so alone?

You're sitting there, smiling and laughing but the memories swamp your mind and then all you can smell is his cologne.

The demon, that is him, reappears in the room and you realise that in this world, no matter who you come to meet, you will always truly be alone.

Why me?

Will I ever recover?

The Most Beautiful Narcissist

. . . .

I'm happy with you being my life. I'm happy with seeing you every day. I'm happy seeing you smile and feeling you when you're not with me every day. I'm happy planning my life with you every day. I'm happy risking opening up the pain of having children with you every day. I'm happy with planning a thousand and one trips with you every day. I'm happy making love to you every day.

I'm not happy not being with you. I'm not happy with you not being mine.

I'm sad without you.

I don't want to be sad anymore.

I'm happy with you being my wife one day. So trust me. I'm happy with you being my girlfriend today.

I'm ready for a label. I want one.

I want everything with you. I'm ready to be everything for you.

I'm not looking at anyone else nor want to be with anyone else. Just don't you dare say you're going to leave me now because you're protecting yourself from me hurting you. I'd never ever EVER fucking hurt you. If you need to leave, leave because you don't love me or leave me because you've found someone else. Leave me because you can't take how damaged I am inside. But never EVER leave me because you think I'd hurt you. That makes me angry. If you really knew how much I loved you/or if anyone ever hurt you I'd pray for them. I'm never hurting you.

You give me butterflies every day. I have so many plans I'm looking forward to with you. No one is hurting you ever again. Especially me.

And the next day, little did I know, he said the same to her.

Northern Lights

I see the Northern Lights in your eyes.

Constellations

You are a map of beautiful constellations. Each star symbolises your courage, strength and beauty. You are made up of stars and you will shine. You will shine so bright, believe me. You just have to be brave enough to know when others will block your light.

Three Words

. . . .

I asked him to describe me in three words after we were going through a break or a rough patch, however one may call it. He said, "Damaged, paranoid and beautiful."

He then laughed and said, "I am joking, baby. You are beautiful, sexy and gorgeous."

Then he grabbed my breasts, kissed my neck and then went on his phone and hid it as usual.

Three Days

So I blocked him for three days. Not once did I hear from him, not once did he show and turns out he slept with someone else. Then asked for me back and denied it.

If only this was a fairytale and I walked away and found my prince charming. Instead I stayed and the rest is too dark to tell.

Waterstones

· ·

The sound I hear on my walk of the waves crashing upon
the shore,
And the sound of people's chatter in the cafe or the faint
music through my earphones,

All of these different sounds that I hear in my favourite
bookstore,
The different sounds that are heard, sitting in the same
corner in my local Waterstones.

I got to know the lady that always fills the shelves up
with books,
And the young man at the counter who always gives me
a friendly smile.
I always reassure them that I am not as lonely as it looks,
In fact the books make me feel whole and I like to stay
here for a while.

Before I have to leave the bookstore and go out into the
streets,
Where money controls us and the stress and anxiety
consume me.
I have to spend all my money to survive, my purse filled
with receipts,
When the Waterstones bookstore is where I wish I could
stay, feeling free.

I believe getting lost in a book can make us discover
ourselves;
Who knew that this bookstore could make us feel so
whole?
So I wish to write a book and it, too, be up on those
shelves,
To make others feel lost in another world and it bring life
to their soul.

Library

. . . .

Your mind is a library, full of many stories,
filled with heartbreak, love, hopeful happy-ever-afters
and dreams.

It is a beautiful creation, so raw, and when you tell your
stories that are held in your mind, you will entertain,
inspire and make a wonderful impact on all who shall
read, listen and absorb.

Your mind, heart and soul is a magnificent library,
filled with never-ending amounts of emotions, feelings
and thoughts.

I aim to visit as many libraries in my lifetime as I can and
listen and understand every story I hear; perhaps you
should too?

Scrapbook

I have come to realise my photo will be replaced or thrown out in many people's scrapbooks. The scrapbook of their lives.

I now wonder if there will ever be a scrapbook where my photo will remain?

Walls

I am talking to the walls,
But they are not listening.

I am screaming at the walls,
But they are not helping at all.

I am trying to find my voice,
But they are trapped within these four walls.

I am trapped within these walls,
But I am going to make my escape.

Maybe not today,
Maybe not tomorrow,
One day...

Blood & Water

They say that blood is thicker than water,
However this water is thick and the blood is very thin.

I find it hard to accept that blood,
As when I'm cut and need help it does not come to offer
help.

I find it hard to love that blood,
As when I'm broken it doesn't offer to help mend me.

I find it hard to want that blood,
When the water being offered to me is pure and
refreshing.

I find it hard to sacrifice happiness for that blood,
When the water cleanses my soul, my heart and body.

They say that blood is thicker than water,
But I'm better in a pool of water, the same water that this
blood I am referring to won't accept.

This House

. . . .

This house is cold when it should be warm.
This house is full but it feels empty.

This house is filled with anger and hate when it should
be filled with love and comfort.
This house is big but it feels tiny and I can't breathe.

This house is full of lies and betrayal when it should be
safe and loyal.
This house is occupied by many residents but I am so
alone.

This house is rotten and toxic when it should be clean
and healthy.
This house is a house but it is certainly not a home.

I do not belong in this house.

Itch

. . . .

I can't help but itch my skin
Every inch, every centimetre

After all I'd rather have you locked away under my finger
nails than traces of your inhumanity roaming free all
over my skin.

My Darling, I Am So Sorry

My darling, I am so sorry,
I am so sorry you felt alone.
My darling, I am so sorry,
I am so sorry I left you on your own.

I just went to the shops
I was as quick as I could be.
If I knew what would have happened,
If I knew what I was about to see...

You will never be forgotten,
but you are now gone.
No matter how hard I try,
I don't think I can go on.

I guess they are all right,
When they say life is short.
But I don't think I can go on,
Living without your support.

I am sorry I didn't help you,
Or know the demons in your mind.
I wish people put the action into
The trending hashtag 'be kind'.

Maybe if people were more careful,
And filtered what they say...
You wouldn't have gone and left us,
On this awful month of May.

I miss you more than you will ever know,
And you will forever and always be my ever glow.
My love for you will never end,
You will always truly be my best friend.

My darling, I am so sorry, I am so sorry you felt alone.
My darling, I am so sorry, I didn't look on the search history
on your phone.
My darling, I am so sorry, maybe if I looked sooner, I would
have known.
My darling, I am so sorry, I left you alone and now I am laying
flowers at your gravestone.

My friend, my love, my darling, I am so sorry, I hope up there
you no longer feel alone.

Words

. . . .

The art of language and our words, they can be so dangerous but beautiful too, can't they?
When did we stop thinking about the impact of our words and the meaning of our language?

Let us use this gift of language and let us use our voice, wisely.
Let us change the world, it is needed.

Dictionary

· ·

His brain was a scrambled-up dictionary.

He was so damaged he could no longer deal with his emotions. His heart was so afraid of breaking, so to protect itself, it scrambled up his words which meant he couldn't express the love he felt for her.

Or at least that was the excuse he made and she naively believed.

If Only

. . . .

She was the kind of girl that deserved to find love and friendship in such a magical way.

Her Skin

As he kissed her and said she was gorgeous, she hid her face in his neck and told him not to look at her.

She was ashamed of the bumps and spots on her chin and carried pain from the trauma that lies beneath her skin.

Blind

· ·

The world is falling apart and we remain blind,
In the year of 2020 we have shown that we can fight.
Fight for our human rights, fight for equality,
But all we are focusing on is the fight for mankind.

The world is falling apart and we remain well and truly
blind,
In the year of 2020, Mother Nature showed us she
needed rest.
Our cities were filled with wildlife, our canal waters
crystal clear,
As the Covid-19 pandemic caused us humans to stay
inside.

The world is falling apart and we remain well and truly blind,
In the year of 2020, we had two months of super-hot sun.
Yet when we fled to our beaches and polluted our oceans,
the consequences of climate change are at an all-time high.

The world is falling apart and we remain so fucking blind,
In the year of 2020, we lived through a pandemic and a historic revolution.
Yet whilst we are fighting for equality and for all humans to live free,
We are destroying our entire planet and all that it can be.
So when you are destroying the planet and when you are polluting our sea,
Please remember, there is no planet B.

Sp ace

. . . .

The stars, the moon, the planets, the atmosphere, the many galaxies.
What an incredible creation.

How small we are on this huge planet, this huge galaxy, yet we always say 'small world'.
It is not the world that is small, it is the sp ace we get comfortable with.

Go and explore the huge mass of space we have been blessed with.

I would if the world wasn't so dangerous...

Treasure Chest of Gold

. . . .

They say it is better to have loved,
Than never have loved at all.
But I can't bear to think of a life without you,
And I can't do anything but fall.

Without you I fall into a dark empty hole,
Where I break every single one of my bones.
It was that moment I realised, as my bones were breaking,
That this time it wasn't 'sticks and stones'.

All my dreams and desires faded away,
And I realised I am no longer free.
Life is nothing like we pictured it and
Love was much harder than I thought it would be.

I saw the cracks in my ribs as I fell,
I know I'm hurting and I just need you to hold.
I never told you but if you are listening,
You were and still are my treasure chest of gold.

Do You?

. . . .

Do you ever think about me when you're laying next to
them?
It is OK if you do, you can't help who you love.

Do you ever wish we were not afraid to be ourselves?
I know that I pray I find courage and the truth sets us
free.

Crazy

It is crazy how life works out and how the paths we
follow,
are never just straight and fairly simple.
Instead: a maze of paths, some with thorns and spikes,
Others slippery but all dangerous and scary.

Is it crazy that I can't get my head around the fact,
That all I feel is darkness when I should be happy I am
alive.
I just have a mind and soul filled with heartbreak,
trauma and sadness.
So forgive me, my love; I have crazy trust issues, I am
sorry?

Memory

. . . .

The traces of your fingerprints will remain on my skin
whilst your presence will spoon me at night.

Labels

· ·

Why do we have to be so quick to label someone?

Who gives a shit if you are black, white, Asian, Chinese,

gay, straight, bi-sexual, pan-sexual?

Why do we have to treat others differently?

Who gives a shit where you come from and how much

paper you have in the bank?

Why do we have to feel scared of being a label?

Who gives a shit if you don't fit into one category,

we don't belong in one box.

Stickers

. . . .

I don't think you ever really get over heartbreak. I think it might actually hurt more every time. However, I do think that you realise more, each time, that you will come out stronger and you will be OK.

That this feeling of heartbreak that can be described as drowning or crashing, even, will go. The feeling that your heart is shattering across the floor filled with your tears, will go as you heal in time.

But it will never get easier and you will forever feel heartbreak until you take your last breath on this earth.

After all, Heartbreak is like a sticker. It is stuck to your chest and when you rip it off it fucking stings.

Colours

. . . .

We are all colours. Colours that change depending on the thoughts inside our mind, the feelings in our heart and the sensations in our soul. We are not just black and white, even though sometimes we wish we were. The truth is we are much more complicated than just a white sheet of paper with our life story written in clear black ink, filling the page with our dreams, aspirations, adventures and journeys. We are a canvas filled with colour, smeared like a marble effect. The colours blur into others, causing some of the paints to mix, creating different shades. The paint brush is sweeping the canvas in different directions causing different textures and patterns.

In time our canvas becomes full and we need to move onto another, a clear one with no colour, texture nor patterns and we start a new painting, a new piece of art. Often, we may feel like our canvas has room for more colours, patterns and textures but others disagree; after all, it is about perspective. So they then move onto another canvas, a clean one, to create a fresh piece of art that the new canvas can provide. So they leave yours behind to create a new piece of art and a journey your canvas can no longer provide. It doesn't mean they will forget the essence of that canvas, the beauty and journey it tells. They may frame it and put it proudly on display or keep its memories locked in their heart or fold it up tightly and keep it in the back of their mind but they still move on and they will no longer add colour to that canvas.

We are all a combination of colours that provides an opportunity for art. We create an opportunity, with the colours in our soul, for a paintbrush to use to create different patterns and textures onto many canvases that will create a gallery of art. A magical gallery that will tell a thousand stories.

We are all colours. Colours that change depending on the thoughts inside our mind, the feelings in our heart and the sensations in our soul.

Rainbow

· ·

Make your life a fucking rainbow and **be the artist of your life**.

Paintbrush

I want to belong.

Just like a paintbrush belongs with the beautifully colourful paints which then make contact with the canvas to create a magical image.

I want to create beautiful picturesque memories with someone.

Ships

I sit on the cliff up on the green hill and look out to the
sea,
I watch the ships coming in and going out, making their
way to somewhere else.

I let the air take my breath from my open mouth and feel
the cold winds pierce my skin,
I watch the people of this little town walk along the
beach below the cliff I sit on.

I observe the birds sweep the skies and circle to start
their journey to somewhere else,
I sit on the cliff watching the ships, my tears filling the
ocean allowing the fish to swim.

My tears are creating a storm and I call for the ships to
start coming back in,
And when the storm is passed, I will step onto the ship
and make my journey to be someone else.

Anchor

· ·

I watch the ocean and I envy its vastness,
And the endless routes and the beautiful life that lives
within its waters.

I watch when the waves crash fiercely up against the cliff
I sit on,
And I realise that not even these deadly waves are as
dangerous as some of the people I have met.

I realise my fear of drowning may not be just in the
waters of the vast ocean that I watch so deeply,
But I actually fear drowning in this world and being
eaten up by the hatred and greed that fills it.

I hope one day to escape and ride the waves with the
fishes and the octopuses of this world,
And I hope to find you amongst the turtles and you
anchor up to me, my love.

Trees

· ·

I wish we were like trees,
That stand big and strong.
We are there to bring life,
And supply oxygen so people can breathe.

I wish we were like trees,
Not like the humans we have become.
We are often full of anger and greed,
And are capable of not allowing others to breathe.

I remember watching the news,
Seeing a video that went viral,
Of a police officer kneeling on a man's neck,
Blocking his oxygen supply whilst he gasps, "I cannot
breathe."

Why can't we be more like trees?
Standing together united, in a forest of love and justice.

Where we stand tall and strong and bring life to all,
By spreading love, growing in unison, being equal and
as one.

Why can't we be more like trees?
Instead of destroying the trees and destroying
ourselves.
We can stand big, stand strong and together bring a
better meaning to life,
Where we live in peace and harmony and supply oxygen,
so all people can breathe.

Chess

· ·

I can't help but feel like the world is a chessboard,
And to survive in this world you have to win the game.
There is a huge human-size one in the town I live in,
With the chessboard painted on the floor and there are
huge statues of the pieces.
Now, it would make sense if the world was a chessboard,
Because I have no idea how to play at all let alone by the
rulebook.
Playing by the rulebook isn't really my style but that
doesn't mean I won't play,
So I guess I will cheat the game.
I will create my own chessboard, play it my way and pick
my own players that are on my team, very wisely.

Scrabble

Imagine if all the words we had ever said were laid out on a Scrabble board.

Would they bring people warmth or cut deep in their soul like a cold blade from a sword?

Tears

. . . .

I have been crying for over two hours,
I haven't wiped the tears once.
At least it feels like something on my skin.

Wrong Cloud

. . . .

I now realise you and I, we are the rain.

We are pure, we are fresh.

We are a rainstorm, trapped in the wrong cloud.

My Peter Pan

. . . .

You will never feel alone.

I will never allow the fire to get near you.

You will only ever feel the rain on your skin.

The carefree kid in your soul will never grow up.

We will be together,

Riding the waves, driving the windy roads and climbing mountains.

We will be together,

And we will stay young and carefree like Peter Pan.

Give Me a Call

. . . .

You'll find the right path, of that I am sure.

I don't know when or what it will be...

But if you ever decide it's me,

Then give me a call.

The Moon

. . . .

I wish I could live on the moon.

No one could judge me there.

I'd start a new version of life.

No one would judge anyone there.

The Stars

I wish I could be a star,
Shining bright and watching over everyone.
I'd be able to bring them hope, peace and inspiration.
I have to die to do that though, right?

Absolutely not. Be that bright star now and forever, for
all to see.
I can help you if you like?

New Girl or *Friends*

· ·

I wish I had the money to just pack up and go,
Live my own life in a place I can breathe and create.
I watch things like *New Girl* and *Friends* and think,
Why can't my life be like that?

Living in a loft or a snazzy apartment,
With friends and carefree people.
A home full of laughter, support and company,
Helping each other get to where they want to be.

Instead, I just sit here writing this,
Whilst living in my mother's basement.
Located in a dead-end town and having no friends,
In a house full of drama and people who don't understand
me.

I watch things like *New Girl* and *Friends* and think,
Why can't my life be like that?
I know why, of course: the dreaded word 'money'.
Waiting to have enough to get out of here and start my life.

Money

. . . .

We are living in a world that is surrounded by egos and
social media.
Watching influencers showing the best bits, whilst you sit in
your basement, crying.

We are living in a world where we are all lonely and
depressed.
A world where we text, "how are you?" without caring about
the answer or wanting to reply honestly.

We are living in a world where we all feel alone and can't
make any place feel like home.
Being told to settle down, get a mortgage, a 9-5 job, have
kids, that is the way it is supposed to be.

I don't want to live in a fake world and live a normalised life.
The problem is I am controlled and restricted by money.
So I sit here and write this, wishing for ways to get a camper
van and disappear.
Then I can explore the world rather than being told how to
live in it.

Sex

. . . .

Just when I thought I'd never have that connection with
someone,
you came along unexpectedly.
You're a risk and I have avoided risks since the day I realised
men can be dangerous, harmful and cold.

I never thought I'd find myself biting my lip uncontrollably,
as I imagine your touch on me, firm yet eventually protective.
Being deep within me, discovering me and I discovering
you and all that lies beneath that persona you have hidden
behind. I can tell it makes you feel sad, alone and as if you
don't truly belong anywhere or with anyone at a special,
deep, meaningful level. I see it hidden so tightly inside, kept
tucked away behind those mysterious eyes.

Your eyes make my mind curious, my body hot and my soul
wild.
So then in my mind, I'm touching you whilst searching the
many layers and walls you have. I on top of you, or you on
top of me, all the pain hidden beyond that confident skin,
beyond those eyes that are irresistible, will disappear for at
least a short while.

I know you'd most likely be rough, tough, wild – after all, that's what goes with that persona, right? Yet I'd be sure to make you feel the actual passion that you need, that you most likely have never got, yet you deserve.

For perhaps, I wonder, you could maybe be the one to show me that not all men are to be feared.

For perhaps, I wonder, you could be the one that makes me have the endless amounts of orgasms one seeks in life (let's not hide the truth).

That is a risk worth taking, don't you think?

It could go wrong of course, but is it bad that I'm not afraid to have you?
The thought of you being inside me, makes me feel good...
so I guess the only thing to do is find out. After all, I think you may be a damaged soul too. Perhaps that's why I know I shouldn't resist.

Lust

. . . .

The four-letter word that one can find easy to feel but hard to expand.

Feel

· ·

Do you ever feel like your heart is too big to ever be full?

Do you ever feel like your soul is too sensitive to ever feel whole?

Perhaps the issue is that you have come to the point where you realise no one will ever make you feel whole and full because they are not capable of feeling things at the level you do.

Whilst he can fall asleep next to your timid self whose tears have soaked the pillow but after all, how would he feel the wetness from the other side of the bed, in which he lies without a care...

You feel as though you are better alone for only you know the pain that one can carry when they feel every emotion with the deepest of depths. The thought of you being too fragile for this dark world tears you apart every minute of the day but every second of the night.

．

· ·

The world has gone mad.
The planet is dying.
No one listens to you.
You feel like there is nothing you can do about it.

We sit on our beaches and pollute our oceans.
We eat our animals or lock them in cages.
We are being eaten up by greed.
We are not looking after our planet.

You don't want to turn on the news.
They only show you what they want you to see.
We are all suffering from modern loneliness and
depression.
The world's gone mad and you know it.

You want to scream.
You want to get off.
You want to start over.
You want to end the pain.

A man holds a microphone trying to say something.

A girl sits on the streets, homeless.

A teenager wants to make some money, whatever way they can.

A group are angry and form a gang.

Everyone wants to be somebody.

You want to be brave.

You want to be beautiful.

You want to be powerful.

You want to be the greatest.

Everyone wants to be somebody.

We need someone to save us.

We need to not allow them to fuck with us.

We need to make a change.

We need to fix this mad world we are living in.

The world has gone mad.

!

· ·

The exclamation mark, what a wonderful thing.
It's no longer needed, or if it is used, it is rarely in the
correct way.

We have gifs and emojis now, that have taken its place;
English grammar and punctuation, will it disappear
without any trace?

Let's hope not.

?

. . . .

Sometimes I question my very existence.

Do you?

Fine Print

. . . .

Trust your journey they all say,

But I can't.

If you read the fine print of the contract of my life,

You'd understand.

Losing Sleep

Take a breath, fill those lungs up,
Close your eyes, set your soul free.

Unclog your mind, even for a minute, love,
There is no sense of losing sleep.

Take a moment, think of who you want to be,
Make a list, love, of all the things you want to see.

Don't listen to anyone else, do what you want to do,
There is no sense of losing sleep.

Firework

· ·

I have always said that when I die,
I want a firework display to remember me by.
A lot of people have always asked me why,
And if it's because I like the way they look in the sky.

My answer is no, although I do agree,
How pretty they are, so wild, so free.
They shoot even higher than the tallest tree,
Oh what a beautiful way it would, to be.

They ignite a light deep inside my soul,
When my mind is as dark as pits of coal.
I genuinely believe fireworks play an important role,
For when you are empty, they make you feel whole.

The way they light up the darkness of the night,
And fill it with multi-coloured shades of light.

That's exactly what I need to continue to fight,
To survive in a world that is not so bright.

When you watch a fireworks display,
All your fears and troubles seem to go away.
And now your soul is filled with colour instead of grey,
Allowing you to be in the world for another day.

I have always said that when I die,
I want a firework display to remember me by.
The answer is, I don't know exactly why,
I guess it is just a beautiful way to say... goodbye.

Notes

· ·

I'd be a liar if I said I hadn't wrote a million notes,
To leave behind for someone to read when I leave the
world.

I have so many because it changes every time,
Especially the part I explain why I felt the need to leave
the world.

I guess it's a cry out for help when the words are stuck in
my throat,
I'd be a liar if I said that isn't why I wrote a million notes.

So I could find the words to say that would get me the
help to stay in this world,
I just pray you look in the top drawer of my desk, where I
keep my millions of notes.

Heal

I know it takes time to heal but what if we don't have time?
I know it takes time to heal but what if I pretend as though everything is fine?

The truth is I am finding it hard to survive and I am hoping to find some kind of 'fate'
I guess that is because I am not strong enough to just sit around and wait.

To sit in sadness, alone and scared, to wait for me to heal and to wait for me to feel,
I guess my scars are taking longer than I expected for them to well and truly heal.

A Barbed Wire Heart

. . . .

Life is a ball of barbed wire and the heart is in the centre,
So it takes time and patience to cut away the wire to get
to the heart.

So I guess I will sit here with a chest filled full of pliers
and scissors,
The best I can find, and I will start cutting away, day by
day.

However, my heart is the same, surrounded by barbed
wire and thorns.
That are all scrambled up and entwined together from
the trauma I have faced.

The suffering and pain I have felt has caused the barbed
wire to cut sharper than ever,
I guess I just hope you are sat there with pliers too,
prepared to start cutting away, day by day.

This Doesn't Have a Title

. . . .

The truth is I don't think I am meant to feel good,
Or try to pretend like everything is as it should.

I think I am meant to be feel sad,
And that is OK, perhaps that isn't so bad?

For I think, for one to truly heal,
You need your soul to completely and deeply feel.

Feel all that is inside you, buried deep in your soul,
So I guess for me to survive all of that is my ultimate
goal.

"Help me," she screamed.

No one listened.

Jumbled

. . . .

I remember going to jumble sales all the time when I was
a kid,
Looking at all the scraps and random items that were
once part of someone's life.
They were laid out across tables or blankets on the
grass,
The boots of cars open, filled with the bits people had
brought whilst they were there.

They were trading their items or selling theirs, using the
money to buy someone else's scraps,
The items then going to a new home, for various
amounts of time, before moving on to another.
Well, I wish I could do that with the thoughts and
emotions that are jumbled in my mind,
Lay them all out on the table, without any fear, and swap
them for ones that were new and fresh.

Mine could go to a new home, a new mind, a mind of someone who could cope with them,
Instead of them being stuck in mine when I don't feel strong enough to keep them in order.
Then my mind would be a table of fresh, new thoughts that are neat, no longer jumbled.
Of course I know that isn't how it works, I'll just have to take time laying them out on my table.

Scribbles of My Heart

· ·

My heart's seen things I wish it didn't and I think, how is this
fair?
Somewhere along this battle, I realised it is more than I can
bear.
I lost some of my innocence along the way, now I can't find it.
And I miss it.

Instead of going out partying and making memories,
doing loads of things that people look back and label stupid,
I stay up all night thinking I am twisted,
wishing I could be kinda reckless while I can.
But I don't.

I could get hurt and get some scars to prove it,
But my soul has no more room for them to fit.
The previous scars have completely consumed it,
my life's been nothing but survival of the fittest.
But I did it.

I'm twenty-four years old with a soul full of scars,
With the only thing that eases it is watching the stars.
I do all my own healing and manage all of my feelings
I don't ask for help, no because I don't need it. Oh how I
don't need it.
But I give it. I'll always give it.

I am a damaged soul, I am older than I am,
And I shouldn't give a damn.

To Be Human

To be human is to love,
Even when it gets too much.
I'm not ready to give up,
But I can't beg you to stay.

To be human is to feel,
Even when it tears you apart.
The wolves inside me begin to howl,
They begin to tear right through me.

To be human is to break,
Even when you want to be strong.
So I lay under the dark skies
And feel the pain consume me.

To be human is to be brave,
And not apologise for having a sensitive soul.
So I stand alone, like a wolf
And I prepare for the next hurdle ahead.

To be human is a task,
Yet ones with scars become the most beautiful.
So now it's time to remove the mask,
And embrace the art of my damaged soul.

Robots

· ·

If we are not careful we will all become robots.
We will just be a machine to society.

If we are not careful we will all become robots.
It'll be a robot army controlled by anxiety.

Read, Listen, Read, Believe

· ·

Read me, if you feel low and alone.

Read me, if you feel like you cannot go on.

Read me, if you feel like you are hurting.

Read me, if you feel lost and don't know where to go.

Listen to me, when I say you are a warrior.

Listen to me, when I say you are strong and fierce.

Listen to me, when I say you are loved and wanted.

Listen to me, when I say you are worthy and needed.

Read me, if you are seeking help and advice.

Read me, if you are unsure where to turn.

Read me, if you are afraid to admit you're hurting.

Read me, if you are hoping to find your purpose.

Believe me, when I say you are capable of wonderful things.

Believe me, when I say you are magic, the rarest kind.

Believe me, when I say you have GOT THIS!

Believe me, when I say your purpose is to bless this world and all within it, with your soul, mind and heart.

No Longer a Victim

People always say, ah look, she's a model, what an easy life,
Yet they don't see the corrupt industry we work in every day.
The pain I have felt is as sharp and deep as the deadliest
knife,
But no one will ever open their eyes and see it that way.

You could never imagine what some of us have faced,
Not just in the creative industry, just general day-by-day.
I encountered it within the acting and modelling industry
Yet I know that people encounter this in many different ways.

All that being said, the point is always the same,
The victims of these crimes cannot expect to remain silent.
Yet it is dangerous, I know, but I guess that is my ultimate
aim,
To show others to be courageous and speak up, by sharing
my own story.

Now matter how hard I worked I ran into hurdles,
Yet the best thing I did, was stand my ground through all the drama.
Now I am here for others to be an advocate and make a statement,
I will be watching when these criminals get all their bad overdue karma.

You take our innocence away and make us feel weak, make us feel broken
But we are not defeated and we now stand stronger than ever.
I've destroyed the status quo and showed others to be brave,
Now you're reading this with the rest of the world because I was clever.

I channelled my pain, anger, heartbreak and trauma
Into this to show others that people like you will never win.
Victims of sexual abuse never come out because they get branded a liar,
Well that is changing now and people like you will soon pay for your sins.

Together victims will join forces and come as one; trust me, this is a fight that has just begun.
Now I'm here writing this for the world to read, we will make change by planting the justice seed.

We will no longer be your victims or a pawn in your game,
You may have corrupted our past and at the time our present.
I promise you, your crime will never corrupt our futures,
Trust me, from here my life will be nothing but fucking
pleasant.

People like you never win; you may feel it, but you never do.
I guess the saying is right, you bit off more than you could
chew.
I mended my heart, mind and soul, put it back together with
glue.
Us rape victims, will use our voices, speak up and we will
always make it through.

Rise

. . . .

I am so damaged yet still I rise.
One day I will shine brighter than the stars in the skies.

I am so damaged yet still I rise.
One day I will escape this abuse, trauma and dangerous lies.

Just
you
wait.

Disappear

I want to disappear without any trace,
Deleting all my social media and find another place.

Maybe I am meant to ride solo, do it all on my own,
I can't afford to do that without taking out a fucking loan.

I want to disappear and just leave this country behind,
Perhaps that's the only thing that will free the darkness
from my mind.

I have never felt such darkness inside of me before,
I just need to find the courage to leave everything at the
door.

And go.
Start my life.

I Can't Seem to Understand the Way We Live

. . . .

I can't seem to understand the way we live,
The way we work to survive and not ever be living.
We conform to the way society tells us to be,
Work tirelessly to pay the bills, have kids and get a
mortgage.

I can't seem to understand the way we live,
When we are merely surviving every day and define that as
living.
We seem to just get by and accept with living miserably,
After all, as people say, that's just life, it is what it is.

I can't seem to understand the way we live,
Your life is what YOU make it, it won't change unless you
change it.
You have to be the brave, the bold, the beautiful different
soul,
That people will talk about and mock... for now.

I can't seem to understand the way we live,
So afraid to be ourselves, in fear we won't be liked.
When a connection over the phone is more important than
human contact
And our self-worth is monitored via likes and comments on a
picture.

I can't seem to understand the way we live,
The way we work to survive and not work to live.
I say, fuck it, be who you are, do what you want,
and don't let anyone tell you that you are not allowed.

I can't seem to understand the way we live,
Why don't you travel the world, explore the many wonders of
this planet?
The planet is a gift yet we destroy it, but we'd never destroy
our new iPhone,
Instead we scroll through social media at the best parts of
people's lives,
When really they're probably crying, forgetting what it means
to be held
and have an actual genuine human connection.

Yeah you, reading this right now,
Do you remember the last time you sat down with your pal?
Do you even remember when you felt you actually had a true
friend?
I suggest you put your phone down and let your mind, heart
and soul mend.
We're living in a world where we all play pretend,
And all get in debt just to try to follow the latest trends.

I say, stop, enough is enough; I can't seem to understand the way we live,
Put down your phone, realise your self-worth and how much you have to give.
You have to be the one that makes the change and makes people realise,
We are not here to survive, we are here to fucking live.

Human Zoo

. . . .

You hate me now and say I am fucking up my life,
That following a creative career won't pay the bills.
Well I won't apologise for the choices I have made,
Even now when I'm sat on my bed taking my anti-
depressant pills.

I am telling you now when I make it, I will be on top of
the world,
Even if I fall, I won't be crushed by the weight of your
words.
Yet when I am successful don't come running to me with
your fake support,
Because I won't need these pills to be high, flying with
the birds.

You were supposed to be my family and always be there,
Yet you showed that you would never truly care.

It's over and done with now, I am OK, I can get by in life without you,
I feel good in myself, now I am no longer living in that human zoo.
So whoever is reading this right now, I suggest you get out too,
Live your life for you and no one else and you will no longer feel blue.

Unbreakable

· ·

You are unbreakable. If you don't know it, you better believe it.

Perhaps I am a hypocrite as some days I truly feel like my soul has shattered and I can't pick myself up off of the floor. I sit and wait, wondering if anyone will come and help me.

Will you, reader, help me? Maybe we can help each other?

My Statement to You

. . . .

They tell me to work until my idols become my rivals,
but I'm just out here fighting for survival.

My mind is full of evil and dark,
yet people expect me to go out and make my mark.

I want to be big and successful
but what you don't see is my life is fucking stressful.

So my dear 'friends', instead of asking when I'm going to be
on the big screen,
appreciate I've made it through my depression since the age
of fifteen.

I believe I'll make it because I've got drive,
but until then you should pray that I'm strong enough to
survive.

To survive in a world full of hatred and greed,
without turning into a monster is the best thing to succeed.

So forget all this pressure and people's expectations
and be the right role model for the younger generations.

To do that you have to look after your mind, heart and soul
and be strong enough to break from your inner demons'
control.

So whoever is listening, you have to be brave
and never ever be society's slave.

Trust the path and journey you take
and trust you are strong enough to never break.

You will never break beyond repair, so for you,
this fucked up world better prepare.

So my dear 'friends', I'll say it once again...

instead of asking when I'm going to be on the big screen,
appreciate I've made it through my depression since the age
of fifteen.

You're telling me to work until my idols become my rivals,
well, you best be patient while I'm working on my survival.

Forever

· ·

Forever is a long time.

That is why the thought of us, forever, is so exciting.

The hope of forever runs through my veins, just like the blood that allows me to stay alive.

Never

. . . .

Never let the pain and trauma that you have faced
consume you,
Because you are stronger than you realise and braver
than anyone else knows.

Nobody will truly know the battle wounds and scars your
body holds,
But the world will see you, when you shine brighter than
any star in the sky.

They will watch, observe and admire and you will always
be there to inspire.

Hi. Are You OK?

. . . .

Hi. Are you OK? Why are you apologising for being sad, my darling?
You don't need to; we grow the most when we are at the lowest point in our lives.
I used to think I could do everything on my own too, you know,
But even superheroes need a sidekick, someone to lend a hand to help you defeat evil.

Hi. Are you OK? Why are you not accepting the fact that it is normal to want to give up?
The important part is when you feel like that, you know how to lift yourself back up and carry on.
I used to feel like that too, but I knew that life was worth living, you just have to find a reason,
A reason why you should keep going because everyone has a purpose, my darling, so find yours.

Hi. Are you OK? It is OK to have a breakdown; trust me, it is all OK.
If you can't find a reason to keep going, if you can't find happiness in the thick cloud of sadness,
I am here to guide you and find the help you need because it is OK to feel so dark sometimes.
I promise you, you are wanted, loved and have a purpose on this earth.

Hi. Are you OK? Well that is a relief, I am glad I checked in on you then.

I guess all it takes is a phone call, I had no idea you were about to do that.

I am glad you didn't go ahead with it ,my darling, I love you so much.

You are worthy, you are loved. I am on my way, I will see you soon.

Hi. Are you OK? I am going to give you a hug and hold you now, would that be OK?

I love you; this is why you should check in on your friends, it is nice to see you in person.

Life is so short, isn't it? We really must treasure our lives and not take things for granted.

Oh hang on, excuse me a second, my sister is calling me...

Hi. Are you OK?

Drowning

· ·

You say you feel like you are drowning?

Well I tell you to swim with the fishes, turtles, whales
and dolphins,

Instead of being drowned by the monsters around you.

Beyond Today

I tell you I can no longer see beyond today,
You tell me to stop being dramatic and get a grip.
I try to see beyond today and hope that there is
something out there,
Whilst I act like I am tough and I put up my walls as if
that is enough.

However I stand tall and say it is OK to be broken and
bruised,
It is not a crime to often be unable to see beyond today.
I stand tall and teach others they need to believe there is
something beyond the unknown.
The devil will not blacken our magical souls, we will
make it beyond it today,

even if we have to crawl.

One Day

. . . .

I hope one day someone shows you how special you are,
But that you understand you do not need someone else
to make you realise your importance.
You see how beautiful and magical your soul is and that
to share it with someone worthy is a bonus.

Your beautiful soul, heart and mind is filled with so
much magic, it is a gift to this planet and a gift to all who
you share it with.

Creation

You are the most unique, raw, beautiful and valuable creation.
If others do not see that, that is their loss not yours.

You are the many wonders and miracles of the world;
Always remember that you, my love, are the art of a damaged soul.

To Whom This May Concern

. . . .

Your beauty will attract them but your strength will intimidate them.

Your kindness shall spread like wildfire, but be prepared: you may get burnt in the process.

Your carefree soul will excite them but your independence will scare them.

Your love for someone could be never-ending, so pure and refreshing to them, but be prepared: you may get dehydrated from the lack of love they have to offer.

To whom this may concern, be prepared but never be afraid to be the magnificent soul that you are.

Love from, You.

. . . .

The hardest thing to do for us damaged souls is to learn
to love ourselves, for how can we if we think we are not
worthy?

But my love, you are. You wear your scars so beautifully
and the strength you have shown, to still be here to read
this book, is truly remarkable.

You are a miracle and a miraculous future you shall have.

I once was in the very true depths of deepest despair...

Yet now, I am in the very true depths of healing... I am bathing in crystal waters, with the moonbeams filling the pool with hopes, dreams and security.

And you too, my reader, will join me in a beautiful healing pool which lies within an ever so sturdy, indestructible cave.

Open your eyes, mind, heart and soul. Do you see the cave of healing?

I hope so. It's OK, it took me a while to see it too.

Art

. . . .

Art is expression, escape, imagination, beauty, darkness, a bundle of emotions, truth, manifested dreams. Art is freedom of speech and feeling, acceptance, therapy, architecture, music, opera, theatre, dance, painting, sculpture, illustration, drawing, cartoons, printmaking, ceramics, stained glass, photography, installation, video, film and cinematography.

Art is your soul. Art is your mind. Art is your heart.

Reach out to art and manifest it in your soul. Never be afraid of the art you bring to the world, just make sure it is kind, free, wild and yours. Make sure your art is truth, make sure it is raw. Allow it to make a statement but never allow it to physically hurt someone, yet do not be afraid to let your art speak the truth and if no one likes your truth, they can go to another gallery or showing.

Trust your art. Trust the art of your soul. Trust the art of your mind. Trust the art of your heart. Trust that it is beautiful, raw, magical and unique. Never be afraid to show your true art for that is what will make such a dark world beautiful once again.

She Built a Home

. . . .

She built a home in her mind. In fact she built an entire world: cities filled with hustle and bustle, hard work and determination. She built never-ending amounts of countrysides filled with serenity and peace. The grass stretching out across acres and acres of hopes and dreams. She built a world in her mind, filling the places with love and interest as she drove away the shadows, for her world had no room for darkness and pain. She hopes these strong, sturdy, indestructible cities and these beautiful acres of hope, peace and dreams spill over into the world that she is living now. She hopes her dream world that she longs for as she creates it, in her own mind, will become a reality. For she is tired of living in a world full of darkness, pain and destruction. Where is the magic she knows she deserves?

Magic

....

Your damaged soul is fucking magic.

Never let anyone make you believe otherwise.

The Soul

My soul can be described as a row of jars on display,
Like a poem of dreams and emotions, thoughts and
feelings.

The first jar is labelled 'Heart'.
This one is full of heartbreak, lust, love, sacrifices.
It is the one that is most hidden,
And is placed at the back of the shelf and to reach it
You'd have to climb a never-ending ladder that has
spikes and thorns on each step,
scarring your feet with every step further.
However, once you get there and open the jar,
with patience, you will feel the force of my damaged
heart.

The next jar is labelled 'Name'.
This one is full of identity, personality, depth and
meaning.
It is home to all my thoughts, feelings, likes, dislikes
and is placed on the shelf and looks to the other jars for
friendship and loyalty.

194

It aspires to adapt and grow, day by day yet
you'd never be able to stick a label on it for this jar
refuses.
It is continuously changing and adapting.
However, the name will always remain the same,
it is the meaning behind it that will change.

The next jar is labelled 'Shadow'.
This one is full of fears, trauma, tears and darkness.
It is a home to a dark, cloaked monster made of smoke
and poison and the bottom of the jar is glued to the
wooden shelf.
You'd have to be a brave warrior to bring yourself to
open it, for its darkness and toxicity could clog up your
lungs and make you choke.
However, for you to be able to open the others,
you'd have to open this jar to get through to the next
stage.

The next jar is labelled 'Spark'.
This one is full of hopes, dreams, aspirations and
determination.

It is, for me, the strongest and sturdiest jar and could never be destroyed. It is placed firmly and proudly on the shelf, unbreakable and bold.

You'd go to pick it up but you will not succeed as it is untouchable. The one jar you will never have and I will never ever loose.

However, one day, I will share this jar with the world and you will observe my spark and feel ashamed you tried to destroy it.

The final jar is labelled 'Soul'.

This one is full of all that consumes my mind and body. It is my soul.

It is a playlist, an album, a movie, a picture, a poem of all that makes me who I am today and it will continuously grow and expand.

This jar is placed at the end of the shelf, the largest jar of them all as it combines every essence of the others.

You'd be lucky to ever open this jar, for I'd never willingly open it for anybody and might I suggest you don't either.

However, when this jar opens, without you expecting it, you will feel it and it will consume you and that one lucky person.

Filling the air and both of your bodies with stars, clouds,
rain and sunshine.

Might I suggest you keep your jars displayed on your
shelf proudly too, and one day,
you will share your soul with that special someone.
But for now, be proud of the jars on display,
for they are yours and nobody can take them away.

You, my love, are...

The Art of a Damaged Soul x

If you have been affected by any of the themes and issues highlighted within this book you can seek help via the resources provided below. Please note these are only a small selection of help that is available.

National Domestic Abuse Helpline 0808 2000 247

Mind 0300 123 3393

Samaritans 116 123

Rape crisis national helpline 0808 802 9999

Or you can visit the following websites of these voluntary organisations:

Women's Aid, Victim Support, The Survivors Trust or Survivors
(for male victims of sexual assault)

COMING IN 2022

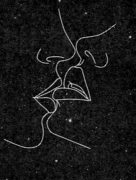

*The Art of a Damaged Soul
Part II*

WHEN TWO SOULS COLLIDE

GABRIELLA LEONARDI